MORE LAST DAYS OF STEAM IN
OXFORDSHIRE

Pictured from Oxford station north signal-box is Woodford-Halse based ex-WD 2–8–0 No. 90066 as it passes through Oxford with a mixed freight in June 1961.

W. Turner

More Last Days of Steam in
Oxfordshire

– LAURENCE WATERS –

ALAN SUTTON

First published in the United Kingdom in 1992 by
Alan Sutton Publishing Ltd · Phoenix Mill · Stroud · Gloucestershire

First published in the United States of America in 1992 by
Alan Sutton Publishing Inc · Wolfeboro Falls · NH 03896–0848

British Library Cataloguing in Publication Data

Waters, Laurence
More Last Days of Steam in Oxfordshire
I. Title
385.09425

ISBN 0–7509–0093–8

Library of Congress Cataloging in Publication Data applied for

Endpapers: Front: Although rather grimy, No. 6992 Arborfield Hall *makes a fine sight as it leaves Oxford with the 5.35 p.m. fast service to Paddington.*

J.D. Edwards

Back: The gradual introduction of diesel hydraulic locomotives onto Western Region services meant that by the end of the 1962 summer timetable, engines of the 'King' class were surplus to requirements, and by the end of the year all thirty members of the class had been withdrawn. No. 6018 King Henry VI *is pictured here on the SLS 'Farewell to the Kings' special at Bletchington on Sunday 28 April. No. 6018 was a one-time candidate for preservation but unfortunately this did not materialize and the engine was cut up at Swindon in September 1963.*

Dr G. Smith

Jacket photographs: Front: Ex-Great Western 2–6–2T No. 6129 prepares to depart from Oxford on 6.5.62 with the 4.45 p.m. service to Princes Risborough.

A. Doyle

Back: An unidentified 'Standard' class 5 leaves Oxford on 31.7.65 with a summer Saturday extra to the south coast. In the siding, No. 34040 Crewkerne *awaits the arrival of the York–Bournemouth service.*

A. Doyle

Typeset in 9/10 Palatino.
Typesetting and origination by
Alan Sutton Publishing Limited.
Printed in Great Britain by
The Bath Press, Avon.

Introduction

I would imagine that all railway enthusiasts have their own favourite railway location; mine has always been Oxfordshire. In the days of steam the county was a wonderful place for a young railway enthusiast such as myself to grow up, being traversed by a number of branch and main lines, and all within a reasonable cycling distance of home. Oxford itself was almost unique as a railway centre with regular daily visits of engines from each of the big four railway companies.

I seem to remember that most of my spare time after school and at weekends was taken up 'train spotting', either on the station or near the northern entrance to the steam depot at Walton Well Road. The general course of events each day, for both myself and many of my friends, would be to cycle into the shed yard, quickly passing the shed-master's office, and leave our bicycles out of sight behind the disused shed air-raid shelter while we wandered around the loco yard. Once every engine had been carefully noted we would then cycle up past the coaling plant to join the other spotters at Walton Well.

My lasting memory of those long-gone days is of the wooden engine shed at Oxford. It had been built by the West Midland Railway in 1853 and enlarged by the GWR in 1862, remaining almost unchanged for over a hundred years. To visit the shed when it was full of engines was quite an experience: the smoke never seemed to drift away and this together with the smell of sulphur and hot oil gave it an atmosphere of its own.

The end of steam at Oxford was a sad occasion. The locomotive depot closed officially on 31 December 1965. However, the last official steam working from Oxford, which was also the last on the Western Region, took place just a few days later when on 3 January 1966 No. 6998 *Burton Agnes Hall*, especially cleaned up for the occasion, pulled the 2.20 p.m. service to York as far as Banbury. Even though steam continued to pass through Oxford until the end of the summer timetable, to most of us 3 January signalled the end.

In selecting the photographs for this book I have tried to capture the flavour of the final years of steam traction in Oxfordshire. The county offered some wonderful locations for railway photography, which I hope will be apparent to the reader in the following pages.

I have, as usual, taken a certain amount of author's licence and adopted the new Oxfordshire of 1972 as my boundary. This has enabled me to include such locations as Kennington junction, Radley, Abingdon and Didcot, all of which were previously in Berkshire.

No book of this type would be possible without the help of fellow photographers and I would particularly like to thank Mike Soden, John Edwards, Derek Tuck, Steve Boorne, Tony Doyle, Tony Vickers and Dr Geoff Smith for their wonderful pictures of the county's railway system. It has truly been a delight to make the prints for this book from their superb collections of negatives. Finally I would like to thank Alan Sutton for giving me the opportunity to compile this book, which I hope will rekindle as many memories for you as it has done for me.

Laurence Waters, Kennington, Oxford, 1992

MORE LAST DAYS OF STEAM IN
OXFORDSHIRE

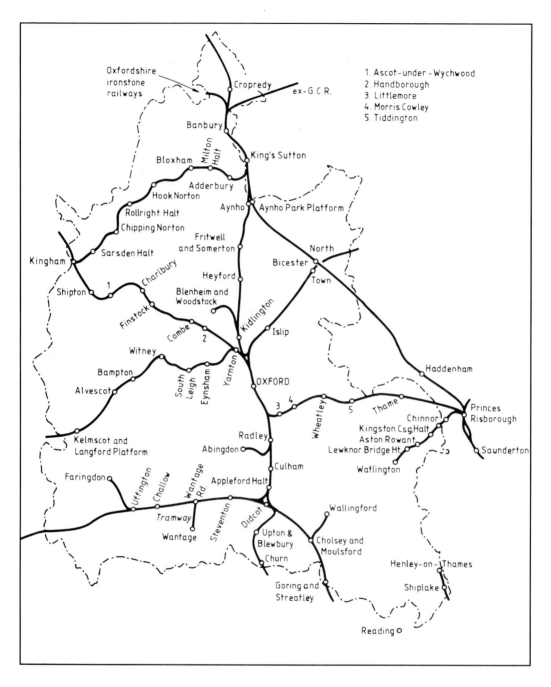

MORE LAST DAYS OF STEAM IN OXFORDSHIRE
(Only locations relevant to the text are shown)

Challow–Didcot–Oxford

'County' class No. 1015 *County of Gloucester*, on an 'Up' stopping service, passes the signal-box and goods shed at Challow in the summer of 1962. The signal-box here was opened on 4.12.32 and replaced an earlier box which was removed to allow for quadrupling of the line.

W. Turner

Landore-based 'Castle' No. 4099 *Kilgerran Castle* passes under the A338 roadbridge at Wantage Road with a Swansea–Paddington service in June 1962.

W. Turner

'King' class 4–6–0 No. 6024 *King Edward I* powers its way through Wantage Road with a 'Down' South Wales service in the summer of 1962. The old Wantage Tramway line (closed in 1946) ran into the goods yard on the right.

W. Turner

Ex-WD 2–8–0 No. 90693 approaches Steventon with a 'Down' goods service. Summer 1962.

W. Turner

Didcot-based Pannier No. 5746 approaches Moreton yard with an exchange goods service from nearby Didcot. The sixteen-siding yard at Moreton was constructed in April 1941; it was closed in May 1965 and lifted soon after.

W. Turner

A young spotter watches intently as 'Hall' No. 4961 *Pyrland Hall* passes through Didcot with an 'Up' freight. Note the 0–6–0 shunting some coal wagons in the engine-shed yard and also the wartime-constructed cover over the ash road, removed by the Great Western Society in 1971.

D. Tuck

Looking in excellent condition, 'King' No. 6003 *King George IV* enters Didcot during the summer of 1962 with a Paddington–Cardiff service. No. 6003 was sadly withdrawn from service, surplus to requirements, only a couple of months after this picture was taken.

D. Tuck

In sparkling ex-works condition ex-Great Western 'Grange' No. 6821 *Leaton Grange* stands in the yard at Didcot awaiting its next turn of duty. It was generally acknowledged by Western men that the 'Granges' were probably the best mixed-traffic engines on the region. Summer 1962.

A. Simpkins

Until the advent of the 'Blue Pullman' diesel trains 'The South Wales Pullman' was the Western Region's only scheduled Pullman service. Here, on a rather dull spring day in 1961, Landore-based 'Castle' No. 5077 *Fairey Battle* passes through Didcot with the 'Up' service. Note the polished buffers, a Landore trademark.

D. Tuck

The 12.55 p.m. service from Paddington to Carmarthen, hauled by 'Castle' No. 4099 *Kilgerran Castle*, passes through Didcot on 20.5.60.

A.A. Vickers

It was the introduction by the Western Region of the new diesel hydraulic locomotives that signalled the end for many fine express engines. The 'Warship' class was the first to be introduced, and I have included this picture for the diesel fans of No. D803 *Formidable* at Didcot in 1961 with a Paddington–Bristol service.

A.A. Vickers

A pair of ex-Great Western Prairie tanks, Nos. 6153 and 6124, stand in the loco yard at Didcot on 19.3.61.

A.N.H. Glover

The large horse provender store at Didcot dominates the skyline as 'Hall' No. 4981 *Abberley Hall* stands on the turntable road at Didcot, March 1961.

W. Turner

A stopping service from Oxford to Didcot, hauled by 2–6–2T No. 5190, passes the diminutive signal-box at Appleford crossing *c*. 1959. Over the years there have been two accidents at this spot. The first occurred on 13.11.42 when a goods and a passenger train collided in thick fog. The second on 25.9.52 saw a goods train derail and demolish the box. The new box, pictured above, was opened on 12.11.52. Notice the sand drag in the foreground.

J.D. Edwards

An 'Up' parcels service, hauled by No. 4971 *Stanway Hall*, approaches the signal-box at Appleford crossing in June 1961.

W. Turner

'Hall' class 4–6–0 No. 5919 *Donnington Hall* approaches Culham with an 'Up' freight around 1958. One of the blue enamel running-in boards that were a feature of this station can just be seen on the right, behind the signal-box.

J.D. Edwards

Minus smokebox numberplate, 2–6–2 No. 6111 trundles through Culham on 2.7.65 with a Hinksey–Didcot freight.

Author

BR 'Standard' class 4 No. 75024 moves past the diminutive signal-box at Sandford with a 'Down' goods service to Hinksey yard in June 1962. Sandford signal-box was opened on 7.4.40 and controlled the newly constructed goods loop together with the sidings into the large cold store at nearby Kennington. The box was closed on 14.12.64.   .

W. Turner

No. 5987 *Brocket Hall* is pictured here south of Radley with a 'Down' parcels service on 8.6.63. The Abingdon branch line which ran alongside the main line for about $3/4$ mile can be seen in the foreground. Spring 1963.

D. Tuck

'Standard' class 5 No. 73027 approaches Radley with the evening fish empties from Swindon to Grimsby. This service was for many years used as a running-in turn for engines recently out-shopped from Swindon. October 1963.

D. Tuck

Radley was the interchange station for Abingdon. The branch platform and sidings can be seen on the right. In this picture, taken on 10.6.57, 2–6–2T No. 6138 departs with a Didcot–Oxford stopping service.

Great Western Trust

Minus front numberplate and in poor external condition, ex-Great Western Mogul No. 6378 speeds through Radley on 10.10.63 with an 'Up' freight.

D. Tuck

A through service from Newcastle to Bournemouth West approaches Radley station on 10.6.57 hauled by ex-Southern Railway 'King Arthur' class 4–6–0 No. 30783 *Sir Gillemere*.

Great Western Trust

'Hall' class 4–6–0 No. 5986 Arbury Hall passes through Radley with a 'Down' freight on 9.10.63.

D. Tuck

'Battle of Britain' class No. 34084 *253 Squadron* roars through Radley station on Friday 11.10.63 with the southbound 'Pines Express' from Manchester to Bournemouth. The 'Pines' had been switched from the Somerset and Dorset route from 9.9.62.

D. Tuck

The ex-Great Western 'County' class 4–6–0s were fairly regular visitors to Oxford. Here No. 1026 *County of Salop* is seen passing Kennington junction with an 'Up' service from the Midlands.

R.H.G. Simpson

The last 'Castle' to be built by the Great Western Railway was No. 7007, aptly named *Great Western*. It is seen here passing Kennington with the 'Up' 'Cathedrals Express' in the summer of 1958.

J.D. Edwards

Mogul 2–6–0 No. 6331 approaches Kennington junction with a 'Down' coal train in May 1959.

J.D. Edwards

Ex-Great Western autocoach No. W87, hauled by 2–6–2T No. 6115, takes the branch line at Kennington junction with a service to Princes Risborough.

R.H.G. Simpson

Although the ex-WD 'Austerity' 2–8–0s were good workhorses many spotters considered them to be boring locomotives, probably because of their uninteresting shape. Here No. 90524, based at Cardiff Canton, moves a mixed freight off the Thame branch at Kennington junction in 1962.
A. Simpkins

2–6–2T No. 4149 runs past Kennington junction signal-box with a service from Oxford to Princes Risborough in June 1962. Notice the union flag flying alongside the scouts' hut.
A. Simpkins

No. 7900 *St Peter's Hall* passes Kennington junction signal-box with a through service from Birkenhead to Folkestone, Dover and Deal in the summer of 1962.

A. Simpkins

New for old! Signalling replacement work near Kennington junction *c*. 1959.

J.D. Edwards

In sparkling ex-works condition and certainly not being overtaxed by the load, 'Castle' No. 7036 *Taunton Castle* passes Kennington junction with the Swindon–Grimsby fish empties.

J.D. Edwards

'Lord Nelson' class No. 30862 *Lord Collingwood* passes Kennington junction on Saturday 22.7.61 with a Bournemouth–Newcastle service.

Dr G. Smith

A local service from Oxford to Didcot, hauled by 2–6–2T No. 6131, passes under the 'Redbridge'. It was here that the old railmotor halt at Abingdon Road was once situated.

R.H.G. Simpson

No. 7008 *Swansea Castle* bursts forth from under the 'Redbridge' with a service from Oxford to Paddington. The signal-box at Hinksey South, opened on 29.3.42, can just be seen on the right, under the bridge.

J.D. Edwards

No. 5960 *St Edmund Hall* passes Hinksey South box and the southern entrance to Hinksey yard on Saturday 24.6.61 with a holiday extra from Birmingham to Bournemouth. One of the nameplates from this engine now adorns the wall of the junior common room at the Oxford college.

Dr G. Smith

A feature of the through cross-country services at Oxford was the variety of ex-Southern Railway motive power. Here on 2.7.60 'Lord Nelson' No. 30858 *Lord Duncan* passes Hinksey with a Bournemouth–York service.

J.F. Loader

'Hall' class No. 4915 *Condover Hall* passes Hinksey Lake in the summer of 1962 with the West London parcels service. This service ran via Thame and Princes Risborough. The lake here was formed during the construction of the Oxford and Birmingham Railway in 1850 and was used for many years thereafter as the main reservoir for Oxford's water supply.

S. Boorne

Ex-Great Western 0–6–0PT No. 3750, with a Southall (81C) shedplate, stands in the yard at Hinksey in June 1962. The locomotive was on temporary loan to Oxford at this time.

S. Boorne

Another shot taken on the same day shows sister engine No. 3751 arriving on a local freight.

A. Simpkins

Gresley Pacific No. 4472 *Flying Scotsman* makes its way through Oxford on Saturday 18.5.63 with the Gainsborough Model Railway Society's 'Isle of Wight Special'.

Dr G. Smith

One of Oxford's long-serving 6100 class, 2–6–2 No. 6111, approaches Oxford on 8.8.64 with a parcels service from London. No. 6111 was first allocated to Oxford in August 1949 and was withdrawn when the shed closed to steam on 31.12.65.

D. Tuck

The southbound 'Pines Express' leaves Oxford on 28.2.63 hauled by 'West Country' 4–6–2
No. 34102 *Lapford*.

Dr G. Smith

No. 5098 *Clifford Castle* runs into Oxford on 27.1.64 with a service from Paddington to Worcester. The 'Castle' was deputizing for a failed diesel. Many services arriving at Oxford were forced to stop at this point in order to allow a preceding train to clear the 'Down' platform, so over the years this spot became known as 'graveyard halt'.

S. Boorne

Probably the fastest 'Castle' of them all was No. 7018 *Drysllwyn Castle*, pictured here arriving at Oxford with a 'Down' Worcester service in 1962. No. 7018 is credited with the fastest-ever steam-hauled run which took place on the 'Up' 'Bristolian' service on 28.4.58. The 117.6 miles was covered in just 93 minutes 50 seconds with a maximum speed of just over 100 mph being attained near Hullavington.

Dr G. Smith

A favourite spot for railway photography south of Oxford was, and still is, the Becket Street foot-bridge. Here, on 28.8.63, 2–6–2T No. 6145 passes under the bridge with a southbound parcels service.

D. Tuck

No. 7013 *Bristol Castle*, minus nameplates, accelerates away from Oxford on Friday 21.12.62 with the 1.10 p.m. Worcester–Paddington service. Notice the oil reservoir on No. 7013 suspended above the outside steam pipe.

Dr G. Smith

'West Country' class No. 34043 *Combe Martin* leaves Oxford with the 'Down' 'Pines Express', in October 1963. This engine was certainly no stranger on this service, spending most of its life at Bournemouth and even being allocated for a short time to the S&D shed at Bath Green Park.

D. Tuck

Newly allocated to the Southern Region from Scotland is 'Standard' class 5 No. 73002, seen here leaving Oxford with a service for Bournemouth on 24.8.63.

D. Tuck

The footbridge at Becket Street provides a good vantage point to view 2–8–0T No. 7247 as it passes through with an 'Up' freight service. Waiting in the 'Down' loop on another freight is ex-LMS 2–8–0 No. 48476.

J.D. Edwards

This fine view shows the south approach to Oxford station. On the left are the West Midland sidings and on the right is the small yard at Becket Street. Pannier 0–6–0 No. 9640 runs through with the Fairford–Hinksey goods.

J.D. Edwards

The cosmopolitan nature of the motive power at Oxford is shown to good effect in this picture of 'County' class 4–6–0 No. 1028 *County of Warwick* running through with an 'Up' goods, as also in shot are an ex-Great Western 'Hall', an ex-Southern 'West Country' and an ex-London and North Western Bowen-Cooke 0–8–0.

R.H.G. Simpson

No. 5018 *St Mawes Castle* accelerates away from Oxford with a semi-fast service to London on 15.8.59.

J.D. Edwards

Another view of the south end of Oxford station illustrates to good effect the station south signal-box and the large water-tank at the end of the 'Up' platform. In view from left to right are No. 75030 with empty stock for the Bletchley service, an unidentified 'Hall' and No. 75024 on the 9.05 a.m. Birmingham–Portsmouth service on 15.8.59.

J.D. Edwards

This view, taken from Oxford station south box on a gorgeous summer's day in 1961, shows 2–8–2 tank No. 7239 with a 'Down' goods.

W. Turner

One of the last 0–6–0s to be used at Oxford was No. 9773. It is seen here in November 1964 on what was known locally as the West Midland pilot duty. This duty was generally undertaken using either a 'Hall' or a 'Grange' 4–6–0.

D. Tuck

One of Oxford's little 0–4–2 tanks, No. 1442, crosses the bridge over the Botley road as it makes its way back to the engine-shed after working the Abingdon–Hinksey freight service. March 1962.

A. Simpkins

All eyes on No. 6855 *Saighton Grange* as it passes non-stop through Oxford with a summer Saturday extra from the south coast to the Midlands. June 1963.

A. Simpkins

The trackmen seem to be paying no attention at all as 'Standard' class 4 No. 75001 enters Oxford on 30.5.62 with a 'Down' freight service from Morris Cowley.

S. Boorne

No. 7002 *Devizes Castle* awaits departure from Oxford on 15.6.63 with the 2.29 p.m. London service.
D. Tuck

Looking in excellent condition No. 7031 *Cromwell's Castle* stands at Oxford in June 1962 with an 'Up' Worcester service.

D. Tuck

'West Country' class Pacific No. 34103 *Calstock* prepares to depart from Oxford with the 3.08 p.m. service to Bournemouth on 30.5.62. Notice the wheel tapper leaning on his hammer after testing the wheels of the coaches.

S. Boorne

2–10–0 No. 92211 stands in the centre 'Up' road at Oxford on 30.5.62 with the return Bromford Bridge–Fawley oil empties.

S. Boorne

Old and new platform-ticket machines at Oxford.

J.D. Edwards

In this view of the 'Down' platform at Oxford in June 1965 the small ticket-collector's hut at the top of the subway can just be seen. Also look at how untidy everything is.

A. Doyle

Parcels, parcels, everywhere. The sign around the station clock advertises Webbers, the well-known Oxford store that at this time traded at 9–15 High Street. The store closed in the early 1970s.

A. Doyle

Towards the end of their life many 'Castles' were relegated to secondary duties. In this picture, taken on 4.7.63, a rather run-down No. 5081 *Lockheed Hudson* moves through Oxford with a Banbury–Reading freight service. No. 5081 was withdrawn during October of the same year, having amassed some 1,208,003 miles in service.

D. Tuck

Woodford Halse-based ex-War Department 2–8–0 No. 90040 clanks (for that is what they did) its way through Oxford with a 'Down' freight from Woodford to Hinksey yards on 21.6.63.

D. Tuck

One of the specially painted chocolate and cream Mk 1 coaches used on the 'Cathedrals Express' set, pictured at Oxford in 1958. The 'Cathedrals', which was inaugurated in 1957, ran between Hereford and Paddington and was predominantly 'Castle' hauled. The name was dropped from the timetable in 1964 but was resurrected, albeit for a brief period, during 1985.

J.D. Edwards

Although devoid of its nameplates ex-LMS 'Royal Scot' No. 46106 *Gordon Highlander* still makes a fine sight as it moves through Oxford en route to Hinksey yard from where it will power the afternoon freight service to Washwood Heath. Note that the engine is fitted with BR-type smoke deflectors. March 1962.

A. Simpkins

The pair-of-scissors crossing at Oxford can be seen to good effect as 2–6–2T No. 6120 arrives with a Thames Valley stopping service. The crossings were installed in the 1920s to help alleviate congestion at this notorious operating bottleneck; however, with the advent of longer trains they saw little use, being removed during the late 1960s.

J.D. Edwards

Ex-LMS 'Royal Scot' No. 46122 *Royal Ulster Rifleman* runs through Oxford en route to Hinksey yard. It would work the afternoon service from Hinksey to Washwood Heath.

S. Boorne

One of Oxford's best-loved engines, if not always the best mechanically, was No. 5012 *Berry Pomeroy Castle*, pictured here at Oxford in February 1962 with a service to Birmingham Snow Hill. First allocated to Oxford (81F) in December 1952, it was withdrawn from service just two months after this photograph was taken.

D.A. Anderson

No. 6906 *Chicheley Hall* prepares to leave Oxford with a stopping service to Banbury, as No. 6815 *Frilford Grange* plods through with an 'Up' goods on 24.8.63.

D. Tuck

An 'Up' service from Hereford and Worcester, hauled by 'Castle' No. 5033 *Broughton Castle*, arrives at Oxford during 1958. The individual wooden signal gantries seen here were replaced by a single steel structure during the following year.

D. Sellman

Not many passengers in evidence as No. 7030 *Cranbrook Castle* moves through Oxford en route to the engine-shed, passing in the 'Down' platform 2–6–2T No. 4149 waiting to depart with a stopping train to Banbury. In the 'Down' bay stands a DMU on the Bletchley service. 31.5.62.

S. Boorne

The fireman of Swindon (82C)-allocated No. 5978 *Bodinnick Hall* poses for the photographer as it passes through Oxford with a van train on 31.5.62.

S. Boorne

'Standard' class 5 No. 73026 stands at Oxford on 10.7.65 with the 11.10 a.m. service from Bournemouth to Newcastle. The engine was at this time allocated to Leamington Spa (stencilled on front buffer beam).

Author's collection

The sight of a 'Bulleid' Pacific running into Oxford on the Bournemouth–Newcastle service was almost an everyday event, but on 27.4.63 Southampton were drawn against Manchester United at Villa Park in the semi-final of the English (FA) Cup. The resulting special trains carrying Southampton fans to the game brought no less than twelve examples through the city; one of these, No. 34094 *Mortehoe*, pictured here, attracts some attention as it passes through en route to Birmingham. The other locomotives involved in the 'cavalcade' were Nos. 34009/28/39/40/42/45/46/50/52/88 and 34098.

Dr G. Smith

No. 6990 *Witherslack Hall*, now preserved on the Great Central Railway at Loughborough, runs into Oxford on Friday 3.3.61 with the stock of the 2.50 p.m. service to Didcot. Standing on the 'Up' relief with one horsebox is No. 6807 *Birchwood Grange*.

Dr G. Smith

Smoke seems to be the order of the day for Banbury-based 9F 2–10–0 No. 92227 as it powers its way through Oxford with an 'Up' freight on 16.11.63.

D. Tuck

'Lord Nelson' class No. 30856 *Lord St Vincent* stands at Oxford with a through summer Saturday service from Bournemouth to the north-east. The 'Lord Nelson' would be replaced at Oxford, probably with a 'Hall', for its journey to Banbury. Summer 1962.

A. Simpkins

A youthful spotter notes the number of 'Castle' No. 5076 *Gladiator* as it arrives at Oxford with the through service from Hastings to Birkenhead in the summer of 1962.

A. Simpkins

The left-hand nameplate of 'Castle' No. 5076 Gladiator pictured at Oxford in 1961.

D. Tuck

Ex-LNER B1 No. 61234 leaves Oxford with the Sunday-only 5.00 p.m. through service from Swindon to Sheffield. The single-car DMU was probably being used at this time, May 1962, for Abingdon branch services. Standing on the shed No. 4 road is No. 5090 *Neath Abbey*.

Dr G. Smith

Admiring glances for rebuilt 'West Country' No. 34104 *Bere Alston* after arrival at Oxford on 31.8.63 with the service from Bournemouth.

D. Tuck

No. 30850 *Lord Nelson*, having brought the 8.05 a.m. Bournemouth–Newcastle service into Oxford, leaves its train and moves towards the loco depot, where it will be serviced in preparation for its return working later in the day. Note the sign on the gantry indicating to the driver that he has a clear road into the loco yard. Thursday 21.9.61.

Dr G. Smith

No. 3820 gets the right of way through Oxford with a 'Down' freight on 16.11.63.

D. Tuck

Ex-LNER K3 class 2–6–0 No. 61817 rolls into the 'Up' bay at Oxford with a parcels service from Cambridge. This service regularly brought Eastern Region locomotives into the city, No. 61817 being a very frequent visitor. Notice on the right the ex-LNWR signal-box at Rewley Road. Summer 1962.

D. Tuck

This rather unusual shot shows 'Hall', No. 7911 *Lady Margaret Hall*, together with an unidentified class 52 'Western' diesel hydraulic, coupled to the Royal Train stock at Rewley Road, Oxford around 1963. The 'Hall' was apparently providing steam heating for the coaches on the occasion of a royal visit.

D. Parker

Ex-LMS 8F No. 48207 passes the locomotive depot at Oxford with a 'Down' goods service.

J.D. Edwards

Ex-Great Western 'City' class 4–4–0 No. 3440 *City of Truro* on special display at Rewley Road yard, Oxford on 28.4.60.

Author

Ex-Caledonian Railway 4–2–2 No. 123, also on special display at Rewley Road yard on 28.4.60.

Author

Ex-LMS class 5 4–6–0 No. 44875 crosses the Rewley Abbey stream on its way out of Oxford with a through service from Bournemouth to Newcastle on Wednesday 19.1.66. By this date the steam depot at Oxford was closed and the few remaining steam-hauled services changed engines at Banbury.

Members of the Oxford University Railway Society are seen here at Oxford on Sunday 11.6.61, cleaning 0–4–2 No. 1435 prior to the engine working the last steam-hauled services over the Abingdon branch. No. 1435 was standing in for sister engine No. 1444 which had failed that morning. In the centre of the picture is the Oxford shedmaster, Joe Trethewey.

Dr G. Smith

Ex-LMS 'Jubilee' class 4–6–0 No. 45643 *Rodney* stands in the loco yard at Oxford on Friday 31.5.63. It had apparently worked in with freight from Nuneaton.

Dr G. Smith

2–8–2T No. 7249, 'Hall' No. 7900 St Peter's Hall and 2–6–2T No. 6154 pictured at Oxford on 24.3.63.
Dr G. Smith

Another shot of the loco yard on the same day shows No. 6970 *Whaddon Hall* together with an assortment of various types, including an Eastern Region B1.

Dr G. Smith

Wellingborough-allocated 9F 2–10–0 No. 92132 stands at Attwood's siding at Oxford MPD on 29.6.63. This siding, which was situated alongside the adjacent allotments, was used to stable Midland Region locomotives which worked in via the ex-LNWR route from Bletchley after the closure of Oxford Rewley Road shed in 1950. The name of the siding is attributed to one Tommy Attwood, a railwayman who kept an allotment nearby.

D. Tuck

'West Country' class No. 34038 *Lynton* simmers in the yard at Oxford MPD on 11.8.65.

K. Davies

The ancestry of the 4800 class 0–4–2s to the earlier 517 class can be clearly seen in this delightful portrait of No. 1450 at Oxford in June 1962, shortly before it was transferred to Exeter. The 0–4–2Ts were used locally on both Abingdon and Fairford line services. No. 1450 is now preserved at Buckfastleigh.

Dr G. Smith

BR 'Standard' class 4 No. 75029, in lined green and sporting its new double chimney, stands in the yard at Oxford MPD.

J.D. Edwards

Rebuilt 'West Country' class No. 34004 *Yeovil* stands alongside the coaling plant at Oxford on 29.6.63.

D. Tuck

'Castle' class No. 7021 *Haverfordwest Castle* stands condemned in the scrap line at Oxford in April 1964. The engine was withdrawn from Old Oak Common in September 1963 and was stored at Oxford for a couple of months prior to being towed to Cashmore's scrap-yard at Great Bridge.

S. Boorne

'Standard' class 4 No. 75022, surrounded by no less than five ex-Great Western 'Halls', stands alongside the coaling plant at Oxford in June 1961.

D. Tuck

The large coaling plant at Oxford photographed on 8.9.61. 2–6–2T No. 4149 stands on the ash road while, unusually, Mogul No. 6367 prepares to remove some empty wagons from the coaler.

K. Davies

'Britannia' Pacific No. 70054 *Dornoch Firth* together with ex-LMS 2–6–0 No. 42970 stands in the yard at Oxford on 9.6.63. The 'Britannias' were being used at this time on the Morris Cowley–Bathgate car-trains; the 2–6–0 had worked in on the daily Crewe–Hinksey goods.

D. Tuck

Swindon-built Standard class 4 No. 75000 stands in the loco yard at Oxford awaiting its next turn of duty. These engines were generally used at Oxford to work local services over the Cotswold line.

D. Tuck

A rare visitor to Oxford is ex-LMS 'Patriot' class 4–6–0 No. 45523 *Bangor*, pictured here in the loco yard in May 1963. It had worked in on a freight service from the Birmingham area.

D. Tuck

No. 6112 stands outside the engine-shed at Oxford in April 1962. Also in view inside the shed is 'Hall' class No. 5914 *Ripon Hall*.

D. Tuck

Ex-LNWR G1 0–8–0 No. 49441 stands alongside the coaling plant at Oxford in 1959. The engine had probably worked in from the Nuneaton area.

J.D. Edwards

New and old at Oxford as 'Standard' class 9F No. 92240 (built 1959) stands alongside ex-GWR 2–8–0 No. 3800 (built 1938) on 12.9.59.

Author

No. 6900 *Abney Hall* stands inside the shed under repair at Oxford MPD during the spring of 1964.
Author's collection

A pair of ex-LMS locomotives, class 5 4–6–0 No. 45147 and 2–6–4T No. 42105, both from Bletchley (1E), stand ready for duty at Attwood's siding, Oxford, in 1963.

D. Tuck

Oxford shed, pictured in August 1954, with an ex-LNER D16/3 4–4–0 No. 62585, a 61xx 2–6–2T and an ex-GWR diesel railcar.

Photomatic

By 1965 the general external appearance of many of the surviving ex-Great Western steam loco-motives was, to say the least, poor. This is well illustrated in this photograph of 'Manor' 4–6–0 No. 7816 *Frilsham Manor* flanked by 0–6–0 No. 9789 and 'Grange' No. 6849 *Walton Grange*, taken at Oxford on 11.8.65.

K. Davies

Many run-down engines ended up at Oxford during the last few months of steam traction. One of these, 'Standard' class 5 No. 73166, is pictured here at Oxford on 11.8.65; it was withdrawn from traffic in December.

K. Davies

2–6–2T No. 6129, carrying the OURS headboard, stands at Oxford shed on 24.2.62. The engine had been specially prepared in order to work the 6.48 p.m. service to Princes Risborough which on this occasion was strengthened with a saloon and dining-car especially for the OURS annual dinner.

Dr G. Smith

The small lifting shop at Oxford. The roof-mounted water-tank still survives, just!

R.H.G. Simpson

No. 7407 stands alongside the lifting shop at Oxford in 1961. The Pannier had apparently broken down en route to its home shed at Carmarthen after an overhaul at Wolverhampton works.

Author's collection

No. 92220 *Evening Star* stands at Oxford MPD on Sunday 24.3.63. It is flanked by 2–6–2Ts Nos. 6154 and 6156.

Dr G. Smith

Looking in very poor external condition, 'Hall' class No. 6991 *Acton Burnell Hall* stands on the turntable at Oxford in 1965, the last year of steam operation at the depot.

R.H.G. Simpson

A worn-out shed filled with worn-out engines. Oxford MPD, October 1964.

D. Tuck

A pair of ex-Great Western Mogul 2–6–0s, pictured here at Walton Well just north of Oxford in 1959. No. 7308 runs in with a local service from Banbury while No. 6311 waits patiently in the adjacent goods loop.

J.D. Edwards

This general view, taken on 27.4.59, shows on the left the ex-LNWR engine-shed, the 'Jericho' carriage sidings and on the right the ex-Great Western engine-shed and yard. No. 2898 runs through with a 'Down' freight.

J.D. Edwards

One of the many local stopping services that ran daily between Oxford and Banbury sprints away from Oxford on 2.3.60 hauled by Mogul 2–6–0 No. 7305.

Author

Bletchley (1E)-allocated ex-LNWR 0–8–0 No. 49377, complete with 'ban the bomb' graffiti on its cab, approaches Oxford Rewley Road yard with a freight service from Bletchley in June 1962.

A. Simpkins

BR 'Standard' class 4 No. 75001 pictured here on the ex-LNWR line at Oxford North junction with the daily goods service to the MOD depot at Bicester.

A. Simpkins

The Great Western 'Mogul' 2–6–0s proved to be extremely versatile engines over the years, being used on many different services over the system. In this shot No. 6309 passes Oxford North junction with a Fawley–Bromford Bridge oil-train on 9.8.63.

D. Tuck

'Modified Hall' class No. 7917 *North Aston Hall* pulls away from Oxford North junction with a van train on 29.6.63.

D. Tuck

'Grange' class No. 6815 *Frilford Grange* passes Oxford North junction with a 'Down' goods service in the summer of 1959.

J.D. Edwards

A fine broadside view of 9F No. 92138 as it passes Walton Well Bridge with a 'Down' freight. March 1962.

W. Turner

Driver Harry Fudge looks from the cab of Oxford-based 0–6–0PT No. 3750 as it passes Aristotle Lane (Oxford) on Saturday 24.6.61 with a pick-up goods from the Fairford line.

Dr G. Smith

Sheffield Darnall-based ex-LNER B1 class 4–6–0 No. 61315 passes Aristotle Lane en route to Woodford Halse after working into Oxford with a parcels service in the summer of 1961.

A. Simpkins

Ex-LMS 8F 2–8–0 No. 48005 approaches Walton Well Bridge on 7.8.63 with a coal train from the Midlands.

D. Tuck

No. 6126 passes Aristotle Lane, Oxford, on the ex-LNWR route into the city with the daily goods service from Bicester Central Ordnance Depot to Hinksey yard on 1.3.65.

A. Doyle

Stanier class 8F No. 48656 passes Aristotle Lane with a freight service from Rewley Road yard to Bletchley on 12.5.64.

A. Doyle

Eastern Region B12 4–6–0 No. 61546 at Port Meadow sidings on the approach to Oxford with the 9.38 a.m. service from Cambridge in February 1959.

Dr G. Smith

Ex-LMS 2–6–0 No. 46465 approaches Oxford on Friday 12.6.59 with the 9.38 a.m. from Cambridge, the penultimate day of steam working on this service. Note the new Royal Mail vans from Wolverton at the rear of the train.

Dr G. Smith

During the final years of steam in the county many special trains were put on for enthusiasts. In this picture ex-LMS 2–6–4T No. 42105 pauses at Verney junction on 5.10.63 with a Railway Enthusiasts' Club special that traversed some of the branches in Oxford and Bucks.

D. Tuck

TO THE BOOKING OFFICE & TO THE TRAINS FOR THE OXFORD & BANBURY BRANCHES & METROPOLITAN LINE

Wooden sign on the top of the footbridge at Verney junction.

J.D. Edwards

No. 5995 *Wick Hall*, on a through service to the north-east, overtakes 2–8–0 No. 2853 waiting on the 'Down' goods loop at Wolvercote junction.

J.D. Edwards

0–6–0PT No. 7445 passes Wolvercote crossing signal-box in the northern suburbs of Oxford with a service from Fairford. On the left is the small loading platform and crane which were used for many years to unload materials for the nearby papermill.

J.D. Edwards

Worcester-based 2–6–2 No. 4113 makes a fine sight in the snow as it approaches Wolvercote junction with the late-running 12.00 a.m. service to Kingham on Saturday 2.1.62.

Dr G. Smith

Sir Edward Elgar, England's greatest composer, was born near Worcester and it was fitting that a 'Castle' should be named after him on the centenary of his birth in 1957. The engine, No. 7005 *Sir Edward Elgar*, formally *Lamphey Castle*, is pictured here passing Wolvercote on Wednesday 9.1.63 with the 11.15 a.m. service from Paddington to Worcester. It was also a nice touch by the Western Region to allocate No. 7005 to Worcester shed. Today one of the nameplates is on display at the Elgar Birthplace Museum.

Dr G. Smith

No. 5057 *Earl Waldegrave* speeds past Wolvercote Common on Tuesday 26.2.63 with the 11.15 a.m. service to Worcester.

Dr G. Smith

Another snow scene shows 0–6–0 No. 9654 at Wolvercote Green on Tuesday 2.1.62 with the 12.12 p.m. service from Fairford.

Dr G. Smith

No. 5925 *Eastcote Hall* passes a snowy Wolvercote junction with an 'Up' freight from the Banbury line. Tuesday 2.1.62.

Dr G. Smith

This view, taken from the A40 roadbridge near Wolvercote, shows No. 4983 *Albert Hall*, on the 'Up' relief line, with a mixed freight.

Dr G. Smith

'Standard' class 4 No. 75013 approaches the Woodstock road crossing with a Yarnton sidings to Bletchley freight on Saturday 2.6.62. The 1½ mile connection from Yarnton to the LNWR line at Banbury Road junction (the Yarnton Loop) was opened by the Oxford, Worcester and Wolverhampton Company in 1854. The 'loop' was finally taken out of use on 26.10.66.

Dr G. Smith

The Cotswold Line

On a lovely summer's evening in June 1961 'Castle' No. 7002 *Devizes Castle* approaches Yarnton with the lightly loaded 6.45 p.m. service to Worcester.

Dr G. Smith

No. 7011 *Banbury* Castle passes through the open Oxfordshire countryside near Long Hand-
borough with the 11.45 a.m. Worcester–Paddington service on Sunday 14.1.62.

Dr G. Smith

The Cotswold village of Stonesfield makes a fine backdrop as an unidentified ex-Great Western
2800 class 2–8–0 runs through the Evenlode valley with the return oil empties from Bromford
Bridge to Fawley on Wednesday 19.12.62.

Dr G. Smith

'Standard' class 9F No. 92007 runs through the Cotswold countryside near Ascot-under-Wychwood with the return Bromford Bridge–Fawley oil empties on Saturday 29.9.62.

Dr G. Smith

'Castle' class No. 7011 *Banbury Castle* approaches Yarnton on Sunday 8.1.61 with the 11.32 a.m. Worcester–Paddington service.

Dr G. Smith

2–6–2 No. 6156 heads a local Cotswold line freight, pictured near Finstock on Saturday 22.9.62.

Dr G. Smith

The unusual scene of 'County' 4–6–0 No. 1002 *County of Berks* (running late) on the 11.15 a.m. Paddington–Worcester service near Stonesfield on Friday 1.3.63. 'Counties' were very infrequent performers on Cotswold line services.

Dr G. Smith

At the same location No. 7002 *Devizes Castle* speeds past the photographer with the 11.15 a.m. service from Paddington to Worcester on Thursday 13.12.62.

Dr G. Smith

The large running-in board at Kingham proclaims that this was once a busy junction, as No. 7902 *Eaton Mascot Hall* runs in with a service for Worcester and Hereford.

Dr J. Harding

Christened 'Betty' by its driver, 2–8–2T No. 7239 passes through Kingham on 2.3.60 with a rather short freight. Between 1954 and 1962 several of these large tank engines were allocated to Oxford.

J.D. Edwards

95

2–6–2T No. 4573 takes water at Kingham after arriving with a service from Cheltenham.

Dr J. Harding

Although the location is well into Gloucestershire, I had to include the following two shots as they depict my favourite class of locomotive working over my favourite line. This first shot shows No. 7013 *Bristol Castle* as it emerges from Campden Tunnel on the Cotswold line with the 'Up' 'Cathedrals Express' on 19.5.62.

A.A. Vickers

Another wonderful shot shows No. 7003 *Elmley Castle* climbing Chipping Campden bank with the 1.10 p.m. service from Worcester to Paddington on 2.3.63.

Dr G. Smith

Oxford to Banbury

Lying a few miles north of Oxford was the rather attractive station at Kidlington, pictured here on 10.6.57. This station was once the interchange point for the Woodstock branch, closed some three years earlier. Here 'Hall' class No. 4942 *Maindy Hall*, now preserved at Didcot Railway Centre, rushes through with a service for the south coast.

Great Western Trust

Just a few miles north of Oxford were the large cement-works at Shipton-on-Cherwell. The quarry sidings here were for many years worked using steam traction. In this shot from July 1968 steam is almost redundant. Pictured here in store are No. 3, a Peckett 0–6–0ST, works No. 1378, named *Westminster,* together with No. 5, an Andrew Barclay 0–6–0, works No. 2041.

D. Parker

In happier times No. 2041 pushes five limestone hoppers up from the quarry, passing en route the redundant 0–6–0 *Westminster*. 9.3.69.

A. Doyle

In this second shot, again taken on 9.3.69, No. 2041 enters the processing plant sidings. Steam continued to be used at Shipton until 1971; the rail system into the quarry was closed in 1974. Today, cement production has ceased and the works lie derelict.

A. Doyle

No. 6123 approaches Bletchington on 6.11.63 with an Oxford–Banbury service. Notice that it is working wrong-line due to engineering work.

A. Doyle

The last main line to be built by the Great Western was the cut-off route from Ashendon junction to Aynho, completed in 1910. The line skirted the borders of Oxfordshire and Buckinghamshire, and in this picture 0–6–0 Pannier tank No. 6421 approaches Ilmer Halt on 25.3.61 with a Banbury–Princes Risborough stopping service.

D.E. Esau

The last regular steam passenger working over the cut-off route was the 4.15 p.m. service from Paddington to Banbury. It is pictured here at Bicester on 13.4.65 behind a rather run-down No. 7022 *Hereford Castle*. Steam haulage on this service ceased after 11.6.65.

D. Tuck

No. 6003 *King George IV* approaches the flyover bridge at Aynho with the 8.30 a.m. service from Paddington to Wolverhampton on 23.4.60. The Oxford–Banbury line can be seen at the lower level.

R.C. Riley

The 9.05 a.m. service from Wolverhampton to Portsmouth, hauled by No. 6871 *Bourton Grange*, passes Aynho for Deddington on 8.8.64. The high-level cut-off route to Paddington can be seen in the background.

S. Creer

This picture shows to good effect the junction layout at Aynho. No. 6016 *King Edward V*, on the 2.40 p.m. Birkenhead–Paddington service, leaves the old Oxford and Birmingham line and runs onto the 1910 cut-off route. In the background can be seen the girder bridge carrying the flying junction of the 'Down' line, which is seen coming in from the right.

M. Mensing

Aynho water troughs were situated just north of the flyover junction at Aynho, so positioned to be used by trains using both the cut-off route and the old Oxford line. Here, on 21.7.62, No. 6974 *Bryngwyn Hall*, on a 'Down' Saturday extra to the south coast (via Oxford), takes water at speed.

A.A. Vickers

A shot of Aynho troughs taken on 19.5.62 shows No. 5936 *Oakley Hall* on an 'Up' freight.

A.A. Vickers

Looking in the other direction, No. 6029 *King Edward VIII* accelerates away with the 'Down' 'Cambrian Coast Express', the 11.10 a.m. service from Paddington to Pwllheli.

A.A. Vickers

Kings Sutton was the one-time junction for the line to Cheltenham via Chipping Norton and Kingham. In this picture taken on 10.6.57 the local stopping service from Banbury to Princes Risborough departs southwards behind ex-Great Western 0–6–0 No. 5409. Although the station buildings have long been demolished Kings Sutton is happily still open.

Great Western Trust

This second shot of Kings Sutton was taken on 27.5.63 and shows No. 5026 *Criccieth Castle* passing through with the 'Up' 'Pines Express'.

Dr G. Smith

Reading (81D)-allocated 'Grange' No. 6825 *Llanfair Grange* is replenished with water at Banbury MPD in preparation for its next turn of duty.

Author's collection

Towards the end of steam traction on the Western Region the remaining locomotives were generally in poor external condition, aptly illustrated here by No. 7917 *North Aston Hall*, almost devoid of all identification, as it stands on the turntable at Banbury on 31.1.65.

M. Soden

Looking at this line-up of motive power one could be forgiven for thinking that it was taken at an ex-LMS shed. It is in fact Banbury, pictured on 27.6.65, just a couple of years after it was transferred to Midland Region control. From left to right are ex-LMS 8Fs Nos 48368, 48673 and 48631, together with 'Standard' 9F No. 92067.

M. Soden

Ex-LMS 'Royal Scot' No. 46118 *Royal Welsh Fusilier*, based at Leicester Central, stands in the yard at Banbury in 1963. By this date many of the surviving 'Royal Scots' were being used on freight duties.

M. Soden

The interior of Banbury MPD pictured on 27.6.65. The four-road brick-built shed was opened by the Great Western on 29.9.08. It became part of the Midland Region in September 1963 and was finally closed in October 1966.

M. Soden

An unusual visitor to Banbury in the shape of ex-LNER A1 Pacific No. 60145 *Saint Mungo*. It had worked in on a railtour from the north on 5.9.65, the train being taken onwards by No. 7029 *Clun Castle*.

M. Soden

A view of the very full loco yard and shed at Banbury on 13.6.65.

M. Soden

'Standard' 9F No. 92203 stands under repair and outside the small lifting shop at Banbury on 17.7.65. The engine is minus front bogie and connecting rods.

M. Soden

BR 'Standard' 9F 2–10–0 No. 92151 stands on the turntable at Banbury on 8.11.64.

M. Soden

A line-up of six withdrawn ex-Great Western locomotives at Banbury in 1964 shows three 72xx 2–8–2Ts, two 28xx class 2–8–0s and a 5100 class 2–6–2T.

M. Soden

'Oh, how the mighty have fallen' could well describe this picture which shows No. 6027 *King Richard I* in store at Banbury in June 1963. No. 6027 had been withdrawn from service, surplus to requirements, in September 1962, being finally cut up by Cox and Danks at Oldbury in July 1963.

M. Soden

The sorry end to 0–6–0 No. 2210, pictured being cut up by James Friswell and Sons at Banbury MPD on 20.6.65.

M. Soden

'Grange' class 4–6–0 No. 6817 *Gwenddwr Grange* drifts past the loco shed at Banbury with a Saturday extra from the south coast to the Midlands. Summer 1962.

D. Tuck

'Standard' 4MT 2–6–4T No. 80072 takes water at Banbury on 22.5.65 while working the Ardley–Greaves sidings (Harbury) limestone train. Limestone workings from Ardley commenced around 1960 when the quarry at Harbury cement-works 'dried up'.

M. Soden

Ex-Great Western 2–8–2T No. 7218 backs away from Banbury loco yard en route to the ironstone exchange sidings north of Banbury. August 1963.

D. Tuck

No. 6014 *King Henry VII* pauses at Banbury in June 1961 with the 7.40 a.m. service from Birkenhead to Paddington. During 1959 electrification work on the Euston–Birmingham route saw a reduction in services from Euston and the introduction of an hourly interval service between Paddington and Wolverhampton which, until dieselization in September 1962, was worked almost entirely by the engines of the 'King' class.

W. Turner

Another fine shot of a 'King' at Banbury shows No. 6019 *King Henry V* with a Wolverhampton–Paddington service. A feature at Banbury were the large electric clocks situated at each end of the station.

J.D. Edwards

'Castle' class No. 5085 *Evesham Abbey* prepares to leave Banbury with an 'Up' service to Paddington, via Oxford, in the spring of 1963.

T. Longstaff

Ex-LMS 2–6–4T No. 42082 stands in the 'Down' bay platform at Banbury on 24.8.63 with the local service to Woodford Halse.

D. Tuck

A pair of 4–6–0s at Banbury with, on the left, 'King' No. 6013 *King Henry VIII* on the 2.10 p.m. service from Paddington to Wolverhampton. On the right, ex-LMS 'Royal Scot' class No. 46157 *The Royal Artilleryman* pauses with the afternoon service from Hinksey yard to Washwood Heath. By this date (1961) the 'Kings' were still operating on top-link services out of Paddington while many of the 'Royal Scots', once the mainstay of passenger services on the west-coast main line out of Euston, were being relegated to secondary duties.

W. Turner

This overall view of Banbury General shows ex-Liner V2 No. 60808 from Heaton (Newcastle) waiting in the bay platform with a local service to Woodford Halse.

J.D. Edwards

Ex-LNER B1 No. 61051 awaits departure from Banbury with the through service from Bournemouth to Newcastle. Summer 1963.

M. Soden

'Standard' class 5 No. 73117 arrives at Banbury with a through service from Poole to Sheffield and York. The engine will be replaced here by Brush class 47 No. D1869 which can be seen waiting in the 'Down' bay. 18.6.66.

M. Soden

The last local service to Woodford Halse, hauled by ex-LMS 2–6–4T No. 42251, stands in the bay at Banbury on 13.6.64. The withdrawal of this service saw the closure of the two intermediate stations at Chalcombe and Eydon Road.

M. Soden

An 'Up' goods service leaves Banbury yard for the south behind ex-Great Western 2–8–0 No. 2853. In the background 0–4–2T No. 1473 prepares to enter the station with the auto service to Princes Risborough. March 1962.

A. Simpkins

BR 'Standard' 9F No. 92120 provides unusual motive power for the Bournemouth–York service as it departs from Banbury on Saturday 4.7.64.

M. Soden

Ex-LMS 'Jubilee' No. 45620 North Borneo leaves Banbury on 4.7.64 with the Saturdays-only Weymouth–Wolverhampton service. Notice the guards' vans lined up on the yard hump.

M. Soden

'County' class No. 1029 *County of Worcester* leaves Banbury with a Saturday extra from the south coast to the Midlands. Summer 1962.

M. Soden

No. 6671 leaves Banbury in the summer of 1964 with a limestone train from Ardley Quarry to Harbury cement-works.

M. Soden

'Standard' class 5 No. 73010 runs off the Great Central line at Banbury junction in June 1964 with a through service from Sheffield to Bournemouth and Poole.

M. Soden

'Castle' No. 5000 *Launceston Castle* was an engine that once regularly hauled the famous 'Cheltenham Flyer' train. It is seen here in April 1964, just six months before withdrawal, relegated to secondary duties and leaving Banbury yard with an 'Up' goods.

Author's collection

Not quite in Oxfordshire but an Oxford-based loco! 'Hall' class No. 7911 *Lady Margaret Hall* passes through Charwelton on the Great Central main line with a through service from Bournemouth to Newcastle on Friday 23.6.61. The use of a Western engine as far as Leicester became a regular occurrence during the final years of steam traction, especially on summer Saturdays.

Dr G. Smith

'Standard' 2–6–4T No. 80083 stands at Banbury Merton Street with a through service to Bletchley. Single-car DMUs took over these services from about 1957.

Author's collection

Banbury Merton Street pictured on 6.7.65, some four years after closure to passenger traffic.

R.V. Leleux

The Oxfordshire Ironstone Railway was opened in 1919 and ran from exchange sidings alongside the Great Western main line just north of Banbury junction to quarry sites at Wroxton and Hornton. At its peak this extensive system was supplying some 2 million tons of ore a year. Refusal of planning permission to open up new reserves, together with cheaper foreign imports, saw the system close on 30.9.67. In this picture Hunslett 0–6–0ST *Spencer*, built in 1941, approaches Wroxton on 25.3.65 with a load of empty ironstone wagons.

M. Soden

Peckett 0–6–0 *St Allan*, works No. 1997, minus nameplates, moves yet another load of ironstone down to the railhead at Banbury. Photographed near Horley on 25.3.65. By this date many of the steam locomotives were in poor condition and services were being taken over by the new 'Sentinel' and 'Rolls Royce' diesels which had been introduced onto the services during 1964.

M. Soden

Peckett 0–6–0 *Sir Charles*, built in 1943, makes its way from the crushing plant at Wroxton down to the exchange sidings at Banbury with twelve very full wagons. 25.3.65.

M. Soden

Avonside Engine Co. 0–4–0ST No. 2 *Joan*, built in 1919, stands between duties at Wroxton on Friday 23.6.61. The smaller 0–4–0 types generally worked between Wroxton and the quarries at Hornton.

Dr G. Smith

The Branch Lines

Passenger services between Princes Risborough and Watlington were withdrawn on 1.7.57.
Pictured here around this date is the terminus at Watlington. Today, although the track has gone,
the station still survives almost intact as part of the Shirburn Castle estate.

J.D. Edwards

The Chiltern Hills form a backdrop to the small station at Aston Rowant, pictured here in 1957.

J.D. Edwards

0–4–2 No. 1407 waits at a rather deserted Wallingford in July 1958 with a service to Cholsey and Moulsford. The branch was closed to passenger traffic on 15.6.59.

R.H.G. Simpson

0–4–2T No. 1447 shunts the small yard at Wallingford in the mid-1950s. The small engine-shed here, sub-shed to Reading, was officially closed on 11.2.56, after which engines were supplied from nearby Didcot.

R.H.G. Simpson

0–4–2T No. 1407 stands at Wallingford on Saturday 16.5.59, just one month before the line was closed to passenger traffic.

Dr G. Smith

This second shot taken on the same day shows No. 1407 together with autocoach No. W174 en route between Cholsey and Wallingford.

Dr G. Smith

Although in Bucks, Princes Risborough was the terminus for many of the services from Oxford. I have included the above shot of ex-Great Western diesel railcar No. W12 leaving for Thame and Oxford as these vehicles were associated with the branch for over twenty years.

P.Q. Treloar

Thame was the main intermediate station on the branch between Oxford and Princes Risborough. This picture, taken around the mid-1950s, shows 0–4–2T No. 1437 leaving for Princes Risborough. Thame signal-box can just be seen to the left.

R.H.G. Simpson

In snowy conditions, No. 6111 waits at Thame with the 1.30 p.m. Oxford–Princes Risborough service on 5.1.63.

Author

Wheatley station pictured from the roadbridge in the summer of 1962. To the right the small signal-box can just be seen and alongside is Avery's woodyard. Today the whole site is covered by a housing estate.

A. Simpkins

Ex-Great Western 2–6–2T No. 6106 arrives at Wheatley station with a service from Oxford on 5.1.63, just two days before passenger services were withdrawn over the branch. Today Wheatley station is but a memory, though No. 6106 is safely in the custody of the Great Western Society at Didcot Railway Centre.

S. Boorne

This shot again shows No. 6106 and fellow class member No. 6111 arriving with a service from Princes Risborough on 5.1.63.

S. Boorne

No. 6111 arrives at Morris Cowley on 5.1.63 with the 1.20 p.m. service to Princes Risborough.

Author

The last steam engine to be constructed by British Railways was 9F 2–10–0 No. 92220 *Evening Star*. It is seen here leaving Morris Cowley on 2.3.63 with the 1.50 p.m. car-train to Bathgate. *Evening Star* was allocated to Oxford (81F) from November 1962 until August 1963 and was used regularly on this service.

J. Hubbard

0–4–2T No. 1442 and autocoach W81 stand at the Abingdon branch platform at Radley in the mid-1950s. By 1961 the little 0–4–2s had been relegated to freight duties.

Lens of Sutton

No. 1450 stands in the yard at Radley with the daily goods service from Abingdon. The branch passenger services were operated using a single-car DMU (right background) from Monday 12.6.61.

A. Doyle

No. 1444 stands at Radley on 16.11.59 with a service to Abingdon.

A. Doyle

The longest-running railway society in Oxfordshire is undoubtedly the Oxford University Railway Society. The society was formed in the 1930s and is still very active today. Over the years all manner of activities have been undertaken, including driving steam locomotives over some of Oxford's branch lines! The following two pictures were taken on 23.3.59 and show an OURS special on the Abingdon branch. Here 0–4–2T No. 1447 is seen leaving Radley for Abingdon.

J.D. Edwards

The OURS special passes the site of the former Abingdon junction station (closed 8.9.1873). Note the wooden fixed-distant signal on the left.

J.D. Edwards

No. 1435 shunts in the yard at Abingdon on 7.9.61. This engine, as already mentioned, had the dubious honour of working the last steam-hauled passenger service on the branch.

A. Doyle

Pictured at Abingdon on 5.6.59 is 0–4–2T No. 1444. The engine is in lined green but notice it still retains the old lion and wheel emblem.

Author

Non-auto-fitted 0–4–2T No. 5818 shunts the small yard at Abingdon on 28.7.59. For many years Oxford had an allocation of 0–4–2Ts for use on freight duties over the various local branch lines. On the left, part of the old broad gauge goods shed can be seen, while on the right behind the signal-box are the malt houses for the nearby Morlands Brewery.

J.D. Edwards

0–4–2T No. 1442 approaches Shipton-on-Cherwell Halt with a Kidlington–Woodstock service *c.* 1953. Shipton-on-Cherwell Halt was the only intermediate stop on the Woodstock branch; it stood adjacent to the A423 (now A4260) Banbury road and some distance from Shipton.

M. Little

An unidentified 74xx class 0–6–0 crosses the Oxford Canal at Wolvercote junction with a service from Fairford to Oxford in February 1961.

W. Turner

Yarnton was the junction for the single line to Witney and Fairford. Here on 9.3.61 the Yarnton signalman is seen accepting the single-line token from the fireman of 0–6–0 No. 7412.

A. Doyle

No. 7445 runs off the Witney branch at Yarnton junction with the 12.32 p.m. service from Fairford on 22.3.60.

A. Doyle

The 12.32 p.m. service from Fairford to Oxford, hauled by 0–6–0 No. 7404, pulls away from Cassington Halt on Tuesday 5.6.62.

Dr G. Smith

Few passengers at Cassington Halt on Thursday 17.5.62 as 0–6–0T No. 3653 (minus smokebox plate) arrives with the 12.44 p.m. service from Oxford.

Dr G. Smith

Not a cloud in the sky as 0–6–0 No. 9654 approaches Cassington Halt with the 12.44 p.m. service from Oxford to Fairford on Tuesday 5.6.62.

Dr G. Smith

Pannier No. 7445 approaches Eynsham station with a service from Fairford *c.* 1959. The large goods shed, seen in the background, saw further use long after the branch was closed as a workshop for the construction of theatre sets. Today one would have great difficulty in recognizing this spot as it is now covered by the large Oxford Instruments factory.

Dr John Harding

Witney goods depot pictured in 1960. This was the original terminus of the Witney Railway and opened on 14.11.1861. The station became a goods depot in January 1873 when the line was extended to Fairford and a new station was opened at Witney.

A. Doyle

The 12.18 p.m. service from Oxford to Fairford, hauled by 0–6–0PT No. 7445, pauses at Witney for some liquid refreshment on a summer's day in 1960. Today the whole of the station site has been covered by a large industrial estate.

Dr J. Harding

Another view of Witney taken on 9.6.62. In the foreground, taking water, is 0–6–0 No. 3653.

A. Doyle

0–6–0 No. 2221 was not officially allocated to Oxford until January 1962 although it had been on loan to Oxford for some months prior to this, being used on Fairford branch services on many occasions. It is pictured here approaching Alvescot in April 1961, still sporting a Didcot (81E) shedplate.

Photomatic

No. 3653 arrives at Lechlade on 11.6.63 with the 4.26 p.m. service from Oxford.

Author

Just over the border in Gloucestershire is 0–6–0PT No. 7445, pictured near Lechlade with a Fairford–Oxford service in April 1961.

Photomatic

A view of Fairford, taken in 1959, shows 0–6–0 No. 7445 standing alongside the shed water-tank.

Dr J. Harding

No. 3653 stands on the small turntable at Fairford, 9.6.62.

A. Doyle

Although in Oxfordshire, Fairford was the terminus of the East Gloucestershire Railway extension from Witney. The small wooden engine-shed here was a sub-shed of Oxford. In this 1950s shot 0–6–0 No. 7411 together with 2–6–2T No. 4511 stand outside the shed.

Great Western Trust

The 12.38 p.m. service to Cheltenham, hauled by 2–6–2T No. 4141, stands at Kingham in March 1960. Passenger services between these two points were withdrawn from 15.10.62.

A. Doyle

No. 4100 stands in the platform at Chipping Norton on 19.5.62 after arriving with the 4.00 p.m. service from Kingham.

Author

Chipping Norton once lay on the through route from Banbury to Cheltenham but from 4.6.51 passenger services were withdrawn between Chipping Norton and Banbury, and Chipping Norton became the terminus for passenger services from Kingham. Here on 19.5.62 2–6–2T No. 4100 runs around its train after arriving with the 4.00 p.m. service from Kingham.

Author

Having completed the run round, No. 4100 waits to depart with the return 4.25 p.m. service to Kingham. Passenger services were finally withdrawn between Kingham and Chipping Norton on 3.12.62.

Author

Bicester Military Railway Hunslett 0–6–0 *Sapper* poses for the camera at Piddington on the occasion of a special run for the Great Western Society's Oxford group in June 1973. The engine was kept serviceable at Arncott sheds for use on special occasions such as this.

D. Parker

Steam Finale

Great Western steam finale! A silhouette of No. 5971 *Merevale Hall* near Wolvercote in November 1965 on what was the last regular passenger working for an ex-GWR locomotive, the 2.10 p.m. service from Oxford to Banbury (11.00 a.m. Bournemouth–York).

Dr G. Smith

Withdrawn locomotives, Oxford, January 1966.

Author's collection